Does Prayer Really Work?

Ralph O. Muncaster

HARVEST HOUSE PUBLISHERS
Eugene, Oregon 97402

Unless otherwise indicated, all Scripture quotations are taken from the Holy Bible, New International Version®. NIV®. Copyright © 1973, 1978, 1984 by the International Bible Society. Used by permission of Zondervan Publishing House. The "NIV" and "New International Version" trademarks are registered in the United States Patent and Trademark Office by International Bible Society.

Verses marked NKJV are taken from The New King James Version. Copyright © 1982 by Thomas Nelson, Inc. Used by permission. All rights reserved.

All emphasis added to Scripture quotations is the author's.

Cover design by Terry Dugan Design, Minneapolis, Minnesota

By Ralph O. Muncaster

Can Archaeology Prove the New Testament?
Can Archaeology Prove the Old Testament?
Can We Know for Certain We Are Going to Heaven?
Can You Trust the Bible?
Creation vs. Evolution
Creation vs. Evolution Video
Does Prayer Really Work?
Does the Bible Predict the Future?
How Do We Know Jesus Is God?
How Is Jesus Different from Other Religious Leaders?
How to Talk About Jesus with the Skeptics in Your Life
Is the Bible Really a Message from God?
Science—Was the Bible Ahead of Its Time?
What Is the Proof for the Resurrection?
What Is the Trinity?
What Really Happened Christmas Morning?
What Really Happens When You Die?
Why Does God Allow Suffering?

DOES PRAYER REALLY WORK?
Examine the Evidence Series

Copyright © 2001 by Ralph O. Muncaster
Published by Harvest House Publishers
Eugene, Oregon 97402

Library of Congress Cataloging-in-Publication Data

Muncaster, Ralph O.
    Does prayer really work? / Ralph O. Muncaster.
        p. cm. — (Examine the evidence series)
    Includes bibliographical references.
    ISBN 0-7369-0614-2
        1. Prayer—Christianity. I. Title

BV220 .M86 2001
248.3'2—dc21   00-143904

All rights reserved. No part of this publication may be reproduced, stored in a retrieval system, or transmitted in any form or by any means—electronic, mechanical, digital, photocopy, recording, or any other—except for brief quotations in printed reviews, without the prior permission of the publisher.

Printed in the United States of America.

01 02 03 04 05 06 07 08 09 10 / BP-GB / 10 9 8 7 6 5 4 3 2 1

Contents

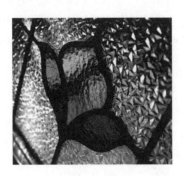

Why Pray?

People have prayed to various gods since the beginning of the human race. In fact, prayer—that is, *requests to a higher power believed to be capable of changing individuals or circumstances*—is one of the most important distinguishing factors between people and other creatures. The attitudes, the daily practices, and the arts, crafts, and music of the human race all reflect the presence of and belief in prayer.

> No other creature on the face of the earth
> prays to and worships God (or gods).

Those who believe in one of the theories of evolution must then ask, Did the human race suddenly take a step backward by conceiving a ridiculous belief in a "God" that doesn't exist? By believing in prayer to a "God" who isn't there? Or did a *real Creator* design human beings different from other creatures—so they would realize that He exists and that prayer to Him would move Him to change individuals and circumstances? Evolutionists should seriously consider this question.*

The issue of prayer really deals with the issue of God. If people believe He exists and can affect both life on earth and the after-life, then it is certainly worth our time to pray to Him. And again, people have done just that since the very beginning of human existence. Therefore, there's *something different* in human beings as opposed to other creatures—in that they believe that a God exists and can help them now and in an eternal future.

For everyone but the very few "total atheists," this fact immediately raises the questions, "Which God or gods do we pray to? How do we pray? Do people really see results from prayer?"

In trying to answer these questions that have been asked for so many centuries, we will look at a book that gives clear and concise answers to all of them—the Bible.

---

* Evolutionists should also consider some of the unsolved "impossible" issues of the evolutionary theories, including the problem of *chirality* in biochemistry and the problem of *irreducible complexity*. Chirality deals with the molecular orientation of amino acids; irreducible complexity deals with the impossibility of complex physiological systems (such as the eye) arising gradually by parts. For more information, see *Creation vs. Evolution* in the *Examine the Evidence* Series.[1,2]

The Key Issues

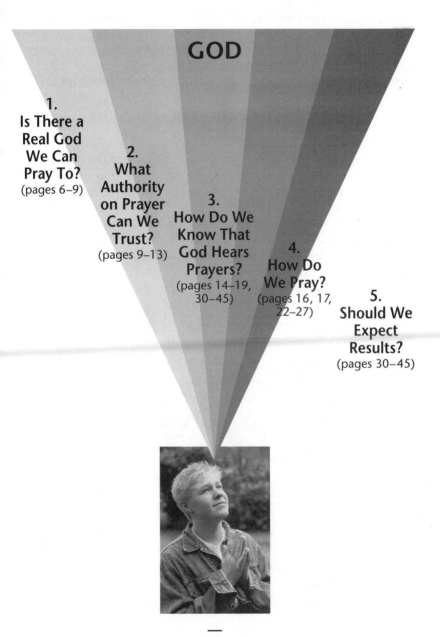

GOD

**1.
Is There a
Real God
We Can
Pray To?**
(pages 6–9)

**2.
What
Authority
on Prayer
Can We
Trust?**
(pages 9–13)

**3.
How Do We
Know That
God Hears
Prayers?**
(pages 14–19,
30–45)

**4.
How Do
We Pray?**
(pages 16, 17,
22–27)

**5.
Should We
Expect
Results?**
(pages 30–45)

How Do We Know There Is a God?

When we ask the question, "Does prayer really work?" we must first deal with this issue: Is there really a transcendent God of the universe who is interested in answering prayer? What evidence is there that such a "God" exists? That He really is involved in human affairs? That prayer affects His involvement with us?

From the Beginning, Humans Have Believed in a God

Archaeological investigation has given us evidence of the worship of God since the time of the earliest human beings—as far back, it is estimated, as 40,000 years ago. (Note that this evidence does not show worship of God by other bipedal primates, such as Neanderthal, which have been popularly thought to be precursors of humans. Recent investigation[3] of Neanderthal remains has demonstrated a chromosomal difference between them and *homo sapiens*. See the insert below.)

Was Neanderthal a Man? Did He Pray?

It was formerly thought that the Neanderthal was a human.[3] However, recent genetic research has indicated that Neanderthal's chromosomes do not match those of *homo sapiens*. They *do* match those of bipedal primates—apes.

Tools: The use of crude tools by Neanderthals does not demonstrate they were human. Many animals, including birds, fish, and mammals, use tools.

Shelter: Neither does it imply Neanderthals were human if they built shelters. Many animals—beavers, birds, and bees—also construct shelters.

Religion: There is no evidence that Neanderthals practiced any form of worship or religion. Interestingly, the Bible makes the ability to relate to God the primary way in which it distinguishes humans from animals.

Did a God of the universe place an intuitive belief in His existence in us in the same way He created specific instincts in animals, insects, and other organisms? It seems so. We humans are the only creatures who show evidence of being able to relate with a spiritual power. Nothing else—apart from superior mental capacity—distinguishes us from the animal kingdom. (Other creatures make tools, create shelters, have "organized" societies, and so on.)

Evidence of God in Creation

It's fascinating to note that evolutionary theories are losing ground among top scientists.[2] Many scientists now reluctantly recognize evidence of intelligent design in creation. Such evidence has been long recognized by those who accept the Bible, which states:

> "Since the creation of the world God's invisible qualities—
> his eternal power and divine nature—have been clearly
> seen, being understood from what has been made,
> so that men are without excuse."
> —*Romans 1:20*

Now, with the electron microscope, researchers can peer into the depths of the DNA and RNA molecules, the building blocks of life, and begin to understand their enormous complexity—complexity that appears to have been designed by a Creator. Furthermore, as we look at the latest investigations of the age of the universe that have been aided by the Hubble telescope and deep space probes, it's become clear that the duration of the universe has not been nearly long enough to allow even one single reproducing cell to arise by chance.

Creation of the universe by a Designer now stands as the reasonable alternative to theories based on chance, such as the evolutionary hypotheses.[2] Confirming the words of the Bible, God's existence and His involvement with humans are unmistakably clear from the evidence that the creation provides.

Which God Do We Pray To?

Since the evidence points to the existence of a Creator—a God who seems to have created the human race for a purpose—the next question is, which concept of God is correct? The two earliest-known religions were the Judeo-Christian worship of a single God; and tribalism-spiritism, which was based in occult practices (not surprising to those who know the Bible's account of the fall of Satan, who could well be originally responsible for encouraging rebellious humans to worship him in this way). If God does exist, as the Bible's account indicates, then it's apparent there have also been followers of Him since the beginning of mankind.

God Is Defined in Many Different Ways

Hinduism, Buddhism, Islam, Mormonism, Christian Science... the list goes on and on. Each belief has its own concept of a god, gods, or no god. Are all these concepts somehow related to the same God, as Hinduism and some other religions claim? Or is the God that we should pray to more specific? Is He, perhaps, defined by one single, very precise source of information, information whose origin is from outside the time-space continuum that we know and live in?

The easy answer, and the one that seems to make the most sense before we give much thought to it, is to accept the idea that God exists in a way that transcends all religions and beliefs and may be found through any of them. But with such an issue at stake, we should not look for the easiest answer, but rather try to find the *right* answer. To arrive at an accurate definition of God requires that we move beyond speculation, beyond comparing philosophical ideas from various religions. We must move into an arena of proof. How can we prove that a God exists beyond the realm of time and space? What can we use to define Him?

A Supernatural God Would Provide Supernatural Evidence of His Existence

What is it that should convince us that we are coming to the correct understanding of a supernatural God? Only something, some phenomenon, that itself is supernatural. Perhaps most of us would like to see some unmistakably miraculous display in the sky that would compel us to acknowledge this God's existence. Yet if this God wants us to love Him *freely*—without fear—and wants us to trust Him for things we can't see, then such a wondrous display would not encourage the free choice to love Him that He wants.

However, this doesn't mean that a God hasn't provided us with supernatural evidence of His existence. If we turn to the Bible, we see that the God who is described there demanded that His prophets predict the future with *100-percent accuracy* (Deuteronomy 18:21,22). He also indicated that nothing and no one could foretell the future except the one true God (Isaiah 46:10).

The Only God Who Can Predict the Future Perfectly Is Revealed by the Bible

Think of it—the gambling industry would certainly not exist today if anything or anyone but God could perfectly foretell the future. The Bible tells us to use prophecy as a test to see whether something truly is from God. And the Jesus who is described in the Bible put Himself to this test. Several times He predicted His own death and resurrection. Therefore, when He died and rose from the dead exactly as He had foretold, He fulfilled His own prophecy and confirmed His claim to be God.[4]

So when we select which God we should pray to, we must first analyze the evidence to see which definition of God has supernatural confirmation. Miracles are one way of evaluating the evidence, but the Bible teaches that miracles can also be duplicated by the evil one, Satan, who "appears as an angel of light" (2 Corinthians 11:14). But if we choose the test of prophecy, as described above, we can see that only one God passes this test— the God who was revealed in Jesus Christ, as recorded in the Bible.

We should seek the God who is revealed by an authority that contains perfectly fulfilled prophecy.

—

Why Consider the Bible an Authority?

The Bible is a basis for belief in prayer. But how do we know the Bible is reliable? Because there is vast evidence that an all-knowing God inspired only the Bible and *no other* supposed authority. Here is a short summary of the evidence, with some examples.

The Bible's Prophecies[4]

One-hundred-percent-accurate historical prophecy provides irrefutable "proof" that a God beyond time and space inspired the Bible. Why? Because there are well over 600 historical (thus verifiable) prophecies contained in the Bible—with none ever shown to be wrong.

The odds of this happening without the involvement of God are inconceivable—considered "absurd" by statisticians. For example, just 48 of the prophecies about Jesus coming true in any one person by coincidence is like winning 22 state lotteries in a row with the purchase of one ticket for each. Put another way, the odds are similar to those of one person being struck by lightning 31 times.[5]

Since these prophecies were written hundreds of years before Jesus' birth (which has been confirmed by archaeology), we know they were not contrived after the events. The prophecies were extremely specific, giving names of people, places, timing, and specific descriptions of unusual events. No other purported holy book contains even a few miraculous prophecies, let alone the hundreds found in the Bible.

Scientific Insights[6]

Similar irrefutable evidence of the divine inspiration of the Bible is found in over 30 amazing scientific insights recorded in the Bible more than 2000 years before science discovered them. The biblical writings are accurate in their references to:

- *Physics*—the first and second laws of thermodynamics, and more
- *Engineering*—the ideal dimensions of the ark for its purpose
- *Geology*—the hydrologic cycle, ocean currents, atmosphere phenomena, and more
- *Astronomy*—the earth is suspended in space, the earth is round, the difference between stars, and more
- *Medicine*—quarantine, sanitation, handling of the dead, and more

The Bible was not intended to be a science text, but a guide to human relationships with God. Even so, its references to science are all correct—though recorded centuries in advance of our time.

Reliability of Biblical Manuscripts[7]

The original Old Testament manuscripts were holy Scripture— that is, a written record of words inspired by God. So vital was

The Accuracy of the Creation Account

Scientists who thoroughly analyze the ten steps of creation described in Genesis 1 find that the order in which the steps are listed agrees with the order discovered by science.[6]

Point 1—When Moses recorded the events of creation in about 1500 B.C., no culture had any scientific knowledge about the universe, the conditions of the earth, or the animals, or how any of them were formed.

Point 2—At the time of Moses, no culture knew the *order* of the events of creation. The odds of just guessing the order correctly (even if the steps were known) is about one chance in four million—similar to the odds of winning a state lottery.

Was Moses just extremely lucky at guessing both the steps and the order? Or was he inspired by God?

the accuracy of Scripture that any person claiming to speak for God who said anything that didn't prove to be true was to be put to death (Deuteronomy 18:20). Scribes—those whose profession was to copy the Bible—were highly respected and had many years of rigorous training. Many time-consuming cross-checks were made to ensure the accuracy of their work.

Furthermore, the people of Israel memorized vast sections of Scripture, even entire scrolls. So any mistakes that might appear were quickly corrected. The miraculous accuracy of the Old Testament Scriptures was confirmed in 1947, when scrolls of the Old Testament (except Esther) were found—untouched for nearly 2000 years. Some of these "Dead Sea Scrolls" date back to nearly 300 B.C. All are virtually identical to the most recent Old Testament Hebrew texts.

Likewise, the reliability of the New Testament is shown by the more than 24,000 manuscripts from the early centuries of the church that are still in existence today. Though many of these manuscripts were not copied by highly trained scribes, there is still little difference among the thousands of copies. Moreover, the age of the manuscripts demonstrates that the New Testament writings were in wide circulation during the time of the eyewitnesses to the events recorded in those writings. These eyewitnesses would not have tolerated widespread proliferation of errors.

Historical Accuracy[5,8]

The historical accounts in the biblical record display both precision and accuracy. In the late 1800s, it was widely believed that the Bible was full of historical errors. But when the world's most renowned archaeologists began to investigate the Bible, expecting to prove it wrong, they instead found it accurate to the smallest detail. Now the Bible is regarded as a major historical source for archaeology in the Middle East. Using the Bible, archaeologists of many different religions have discovered entire cities and cultures whose existence had been long forgotten.

Non-Christian Evidence of Jesus' Existence

Critics sometimes maintain that all written evidence of Jesus Christ comes from biblical Christian writings, and these they dismiss as biased. However, these writings must be reckoned with for many historical reasons, especially the willingness of many of the eyewitnesses of the events to die martyrs' deaths to defend the written record. The martyrdom of these early Christians is supported by many archaeological finds.

Furthermore, there are a number of non-Christian writings that refer to Jesus, His miracles, His crucifixion, and belief in His resurrection.[5] The sources include:

- Josephus
- Cornelius Tacitus
- Hadrian
- Phlegon
- Mara Bar-Serapion

- Thallus
- Pliny the Younger
- Suetonius
- Lucian of Samosata
- The Jewish Talmud

Especially important are archaeological finds that support the God-inspired prophecies of the Bible. The Dead Sea Scrolls (see previous page) are but one example. Early copies of the Septuagint (a translation of Scripture made from Hebrew to Greek in about 280 B.C.) and other early translations also confirm the prophetic text.

One of the most amazing prophecy-confirming finds was the "Cyrus cylinder," which records King Cyrus of Persia's decree allowing the return of the Israelites from exile. This decree had been prophesied by Isaiah about 200 years earlier—long before Cyrus was born (Isaiah 44:28). And archaeological evidence that confirms other prophecies from both the Old and New Testaments is abundant.

Elijah's Prayer Contest

We've seen that the Bible is the only source that predicts the future reliably—which is the ultimate test to determine whether something comes from God. Now we'll review several of the many prayers in the Bible that show how God responds to prayer, before we look at some well-documented modern examples. Of the prayers in the Bible, Elijah's prayer contest is one of the most amazing.

Elijah was fleeing from the evil King Ahab and the infamous Queen Jezebel (1 Kings 18). He was in a difficult spot and was very depressed. All of the prophets of the God of Israel were being killed. Nonetheless, God commanded Elijah to approach Ahab. Elijah must certainly have felt this would lead to a sudden death, but he still trusted that God would answer his prayers.

When Elijah confronted Ahab and his 450 priests, all worshipers of the pagan god, Baal, he sent messages and called together the people of Israel—and proposed a "prayer challenge" to determine which god was real.

This challenge was a test of prayer.

The 450 prophets of Baal were to prepare a bull for a burnt offering; but they were to call on Baal to actually provide the fire to ignite the wood for the offering. They commenced to pray from morning till noon, dancing around the altar where the sacrifice was laid, even slashing their own bodies so the blood flowed, which was a common practice of those who worshiped Baal. They seemed to be certain their actions would cause their god Baal to answer prayer.

No fire was produced by the "god" Baal.

Elijah, one of the few prophets of God left in Israel, facing his own possible execution, went so far as to taunt the 450 prophets of Baal, telling them to "shout louder" so Baal would hear them: "Maybe he is sleeping and needs to be awakened" (verse 27).

Elijah seemed to be displaying incredible audacity, yet obviously he had enormous confidence in his God (something we can all learn from). After all, if he had failed in this prayer contest, Elijah would certainly have faced the same death as had the other prophets before him.

Evening finally came, with no results for the prophets of Baal. When it came time for Elijah to "step to the mark"—one prophet against 450—he repaired the altar of the Lord, which was in ruins because of the wickedness of Ahab and Jezebel. To make the repairs, he used 12 stones symbolizing the 12 tribes of Israel. Then Elijah cut up the bull and placed the pieces on the wood on the altar, as was the custom.

Elijah then ordered four large jars to be filled with water and the water to be poured over the bull and the wood. He then ordered the four jars to be filled yet again and the water again to be poured over the sacrifice, soaking the wood and the bull. Obviously he wanted everyone to understand that his God was real, so that his prayers to God would convince a skeptical, evil nation that God answers the prayers of those who follow Him. Then Elijah ordered yet a third dousing of water. Even the trench that had been dug around the altar was filled with water.

Elijah's prayer to God was very simple:

> "O Lord, God of Abraham, Isaac and Israel,
> let it be known today that you are God in Israel and that I am
> your servant and have done all these things at your command.
> Answer me, O Lord, answer me, so these people
> will know that you, O Lord, are God, and that you are
> turning their hearts back again."
> —1 Kings 18:36,37

The fire of the Lord came down from heaven, consuming the bull, the wood, the stones, and even the water in the trench. After this tremendous evidence of answered prayer, all the prophets of Baal were seized and killed.

Jehoshaphat's Prayer for Deliverance

One of the model prayers in the Bible is the prayer of Jehoshaphat, who became king of Judah (the two southern tribes of Israel) in about 872 B.C. He was facing an impossible situation, with invading armies from the neighboring kingdoms of Moab, Ammon, and Mount Seir (Edom) about to overrun Judah. Jehoshaphat's enemies were overwhelmingly more powerful, with far more soldiers than Judah.

Jehoshaphat's prayer is recorded in 2 Chronicles 20:6-12. It contains many elements that relate to the features of Jesus' most famous prayer, the "Lord's prayer" (see pages 22–27). The key elements of Jehoshaphat's prayer are:

1. *A clear description of God:* "O LORD, God of our fathers, are you not the God who is in heaven?"

   For the people of Judah, this would leave no doubt about which God Jehoshaphat was praying to. This God is the same God as that of their fathers and is the heavenly God, not an earthly one.

2. *Adoration of God:* "You rule over all the kingdoms of the nations. Power and might are in your hand."

   This places the position and role of God in proper perspective—He is far above anyone and anything. He is the Creator of the universe. Jehoshaphat has no doubt about his belief in and reliance on God.

3. *A reminder to God of His promises:* "O our God, did you not drive out the inhabitants of this land before your people of Israel and give it forever to the descendants of Abraham your friend? They have lived in it and have built in it a sanctuary for your Name."

   Of course God already knew His promises, but this affirms that the people also remembered them and were trusting God for the ultimate resolution.

4. *A definition of the problem:* "But now here are men from Ammon, Moab and Mount Seir, whose territory you would not allow Israel to invade when they came from Egypt; so they turned away from them and did not destroy them. See how they are repaying us by coming to drive us out of the possession you gave us as an inheritance."

This problem was completely out of hand for Jehoshaphat, which he stated clearly to God. Notice that he reminds God of Israel's special relationship with Him.

5. *A request for help:* "O our God, will you not judge them? For we have no power to face this vast army that is attacking us. We do not know what to do, but our eyes are upon you."

So often we don't receive God's help simply because we don't ask. Jehoshaphat recognized his dilemma and then asked for help.

6. *Thanks to God in advance:* "Give thanks to the Lord, for his love endures forever" (verse 21).

Jehoshaphat appointed men to sing this to the Lord as the army marched out. He had total confidence in God's enduring love before the great battle that was to ensue.

God provided a remarkable victory. The attacking armies ended up killing each other, with Jehoshaphat's forces essentially just looking on.

More Things We Can Learn from the Bible About Prayer

Before we study some present-day prayers that confirm that God is still interacting with people who know Him, let's look at what some other prayers and prophecies recorded in the Bible can teach us.

David's prayer in 1 Chronicles 29:10-19 shows to whom glory truly belongs. Through this prayer, David—whom God had declared to be a man after His own heart—gave great glory to God for providing the materials needed to begin construction of the temple in Jerusalem. Even though God had commanded David not to start work, but to allow his son Solomon to actually perform the construction, David's heart remained fixed on God. He faithfully praised God for what He had provided.

Daniel's prayer in Daniel 2:20-23—a demonstration of confidence in God. Daniel praised God, then acknowledged His power, wisdom, and ultimate control over all things. He thanked God in advance for the special knowledge that He would give to Daniel.

Hezekiah's prayer in Isaiah 38:3—a request for God to extend life despite a bad prognosis. Hezekiah had a fatal disease that would end his life soon. After a normal period of weeping and self-pity, Hezekiah prayed a moving prayer, requesting and confidently trusting that God would heal him. God gave Hezekiah 15 more years of life.

Zedekiah's request in Jeremiah 21:2—sometimes God says "no." Zedekiah, the last king of Judah before Jerusalem was destroyed, asked the prophet Jeremiah to approach God on his behalf and request a miracle to save Judah from the invading Babylonians. God revealed to Jeremiah that, not only would Zedekiah's request not be answered, but that He Himself would "fight against" those who were defending Jerusalem, because of Judah's wickedness. God refused to answer Zedekiah's self-serving request because He had already revealed that He wanted Judah to repent and turn to Him. Zedekiah was willing to ask for a miracle, but he wasn't willing to repent. Here God demonstrated His love by providing a way out—repentance—but He also demonstrated His justice and holiness by bringing judgment.

Isaiah's prophecy in Isaiah 1:15-17 speaks of God's reaction to the prayers of people who refuse to repent. Isaiah's prophecy is disturbing because it indicates that God detests it when we are cavalier about Him and His Holiness, and then pray to Him like a "genie in a bottle." When people want things that God can give but don't want God Himself, they cannot gain through prayer any of the wonderful blessings that He has promised.

Moses' prayer in Exodus 14:13-15—there are times when God wants us to stop praying and start moving. Moses was faced with the fierce Egyptian army bearing down on the Hebrews at the rear while the Red Sea blocked their escape in front. When Moses prayed—naturally enough—for deliverance, God answered (in paraphrase), "Why are you still calling out to me? Trust me for what I've already done," and said, "Get going!" When God has given us firm assurance that we can trust, we should move out, not "hide out" in prayer. In the case of the Hebrew nation, God acted, as He had said He would, and divided the Red Sea so they could pass through.

Ezekiel's prophecy to the elders of Israel in Ezekiel 20:3—during the period before Jesus' death and resurrection, sometimes God refused to hear prayer. As hard as it may sound, before Jesus reconciled all people to God, sometimes "time would run out" for people to approach God in prayer. God had repeatedly revealed His commands and His will to the nation of Israel, but they continued to disobey. His word through Ezekiel to the elders of Israel was, "I will not let you inquire of me." Then God explained that He had repeatedly told them of their problems and had nothing more to say.

The Good News About Prayer Since the Time of Jesus

Though we can learn a great deal about prayer from the Old Testament, Jesus' interaction with His disciples—and His example of total dependence on God the Father—add a new dimension to our understanding of prayer. Jesus' words and life, and the revelation He granted to the apostles (Paul, Peter, James, and others) show us that God, our loving Father, wants to interact with us on a continual basis.

Paul says to keep on praying for all things (Ephesians 6:18). Jesus indicated to Paul that now we can have a direct relationship with God through Him, and that furthermore we should pray continually for *all* things. That means for all needs, even seemingly trivial ones. God wants a relationship. God wants constant communication with us, and prayer is the method. Again, God is not a "genie in a bottle," but if your heart has a desire, perhaps He has planted it there and you need to pray about it. The amazing, true prayer stories at the end of this book will help you understand this.

"Arrow Prayers"

What are "arrow prayers"? Simply put, they are short, very quick prayers, often in the most unusual places or situations, when you may say "God, I've got a problem—please help me."

God wants constant communication—to be your best friend. He's there. He's available. Better yet, God can definitely help you, even when a friend could not. (He has worked things out for me many times.)

An example of an "arrow prayer" in the Bible is Nehemiah's quick prayer to God in a situation that could well have cost him his life (Nehemiah 2:4). Nehemiah used this type of prayer other times as well (4:4,5; 5:19; 13:14,22,31). Use arrow prayers to call to your best friend—God.

Luke wrote of finding a place to pray (Luke 6:12). Luke tells us that Jesus often sought a place of solitude to pray. (I usually do too.) It takes our mind off of other distractions. However, never worry about where to pray. Personal experience indicates that quick prayers to God in the most unlikely places produce miracles (see the "Arrow Prayers" insert on the previous page).

Jesus prays His longest recorded prayer—commissioning, praising, and teaching (John 17:20–26). Apart from the "Lord's prayer" (see pages 22–27), this may be the most revealing prayer of Jesus. After all, He is God in human flesh, teaching humans how to relate to a living God. There are several vital points to this prayer:

1. He prays not only for the disciples, but for all those who follow God's message.

2. He confirms that He is God ("I am in you"—speaking to the Father in verse 21).

3. He prays for the Gospel to be preached and to be believed by the world.

4. He provides a revelation of His glory to the disciples while also recognizing God's glory.

5. He requests success for and unity among His followers in the world, based on His role.

6. He affirms His own position from before the world began.

7. He requests that His followers be brought to the place where He is.

8. He confirms His desire that He Himself and the Father's love be in His disciples.

James says that we must be patient, waiting for God's plans to unfold (James 5:7–11). For this reason we often don't get answers to prayer when we think we need them. We have to realize that God knows the best timing.

Jesus' Model Prayer— The "Lord's Prayer"

Jesus showed us how to pray. In fact, He said to His disciples, "This is how you should pray," and proceeded to teach them what we now call the "Lord's prayer" (Matthew 6:9–13 NKJV).[9]

1. *"Our Father in heaven, hallowed be Your name."*

Why would Jesus refer to God as His heavenly Father? After all, Jesus was God also—He too created the world (John 1:3). More than 70 times in the Gospels Jesus uses the term of endearment "Father" when speaking of God.

Jesus uses this form of opening as a model—showing that we should relate to God in a *father-son relationship*. Yet he specifically calls God a *heavenly* Father, not an earthly father who would make lots of human mistakes. God is a *perfect, heavenly* Father— a father we can trust. Jesus also wanted us to understand that God is a person, not some type of "force." We can relate to a person. And God is a person who cares about *us*.

Why did Jesus pray that God's name be hallowed (set apart as holy)? In Jesus' time, names meant something. They expressed character and importance. This places the name of God above all names—a name to be worshiped and revered.

And by "hallowing" His name, we are acknowledging that He alone is deserving of worship—that He alone is the heavenly Father and is all of the following:

- He is a *caring* Father (loving and compassionate)

- He is a *consistent* Father (completely dependable)

- He is a *close* Father (there all the time—closer than you can imagine)

- He is a *capable* Father (there is nothing beyond His ability)

The Word "Daily"[9]

The Greek word in the Lord's prayer that is translated "daily" (in the phrase "our daily bread") was found nowhere else in ancient Greek writings (Homer, Plato, or others). Translators had difficulty with this until they found it in the Dead Sea scrolls discovered in 1947–48. It was a word used of shopping lists for perishable items that couldn't be stored for more than a day. Hence the translation "daily."

2. *"Your kingdom come. Your will be done on earth as it is in heaven."*

Jesus teaches us to affirm, with total assurance, that His disciples—anyone who accepts His sacrifice on the cross—will enter the kingdom of heaven.

Furthermore, He requests God's sovereign will to be done on earth, and acknowledges God's supreme position in heaven. Jesus' prayer to God does not make Him any less than God. Jesus and God are one (John 10:30). But we humans can't understand the infinite power and majesty of God. We can, however, understand another human. Jesus was modeling what we humans should seek—complete dependence on God's perfect will.

So what is the will of God for us? He tells us what it is in four basic areas:

- To know Him (Ephesians 1:17)

- To be like Him (Romans 8:28,29)

- To serve Him (Romans 12:1,2)

- To live with Him in heaven (2 Corinthians 5:1-5)

3. *"Give us this day our daily bread."*

Jesus often declared and demonstrated that God will provide for our needs. This doesn't mean He'll provide for all our "greeds." (However, as the following personal stories show, even things that seem like greeds can fit into God's plan for good—that's why Ephesians 6:18 says to "pray...with all kinds of prayers and requests.")

Jesus often used bread as an example of God's provision. Twice He multiplied bread for crowds that were following Him (Matthew 14:15-21; 15:32-39). He referred to Himself as the "bread of life" (John 6:35,48). Bread was holy in the Jewish temple. Even the name of the town of Jesus' birth meant "house of bread." Daily bread most obviously refers to 1) the daily physical provision for the Hebrews in the wilderness and 2) the statement by Jesus at the last supper regarding bread— "This is my body given for you"—the daily spiritual provision for His disciples (Luke 22:19).

Just as bread symbolized the meeting of people's needs 2000 years ago, today we have many needs. A need for shelter. A need for an income. Maybe a need for transportation. God wants to meet our real needs, and Jesus taught us to pray about them. The Bible says the following about asking for God's provisions:

> "You do not have, because you do not ask God. When you ask, you do not receive, because you ask with the wrong motives, that you may spend what you get on your pleasures."
> —*James 4:3*

- *Ask.* Often we do not receive because we do not ask or because we have the wrong motives (James 4:3).

- *Remember God's resources.* God tells us not to worry about our needs if we put Him first in our lives (Matthew 6:32,33).

- *Trust God's timing.* God does not let His people down. Yet He wants us to live by faith—trusting that provisions will be given "today" on a "daily" basis.

4. *"Forgive us our debts, as we forgive our debtors."*

Why does Jesus place such importance upon our forgiveness of wrongs (another meaning of "debts") in this prayer to God? It's because forgiveness heals the guilt of past wrongs and allows us to have joy in the present. But we need to realize that God *truly* forgives us. Jesus also teaches us how to forgive—"as we forgive our debtors." In other words, we need to learn to make the *choice* of forgiveness.

God also forgives *every* sin except for "blasphemy against the Spirit" (Matthew 12:31). What is this? Simply put, it's an ultimate and final rejection of Jesus Christ in spite of the prompting of the Holy Spirit (anyone who hears the Gospel will be prompted by the Spirit). Essentially, it's a total rejection of God's love.

When we ask God for forgiveness, we can be assured of the following:

- *God forgives instantly.* He does not have to "wait" to forgive (Isaiah 55:7).

- *God forgives completely.* The Bible says the debt is canceled (Colossians 2:13,14).

- *God forgives repeatedly.* Jesus taught us to forgive others countless times (Matthew 18:21,22), which reveals God's nature—His forgiveness is unending.

5. *"Do not lead us into temptation, but deliver us from the evil one."*

Jesus understood temptation. The Bible indicates He faced all of the temptations we face today (Hebrews 4:15). Where did He get His strength to get through the temptations that are inevitable for humans? He got His strength from God the Father, as this prayer indicates—just as we must. We are not strong enough to deal with temptation on our own.

Jesus also taught us to ask for deliverance from the evil one (Satan and his demons). We must go contrary to the popular belief that often rejects Satan, hell, and other unpleasant things, once we accept the Bible as the authority inspired by God (pages 10–13 and as verified in the entire *Examine the Evidence* Series). We should consider what it says. In this prayer and in other parts of the Bible, Jesus teaches us how to deal with temptation—and with the "evil one."

How to Pray

There is no set way to pray, because you are simply talking to God. Maybe you're praising Him, or thanking Him, or just making an "arrow" request. (Remember, God wants to talk to you in *all* things—even requests He may not grant—see Ephesians 6:18.) Jesus' and Jehoshaphat's prayers are good examples:

- Pray with passion! Go boldly to God. (This boldness is reflected in virtually all of the Bible's prayers.)

- Acknowledge who God is. Give Him His due as the God of heaven.

- Adore Him. Worship Him. Let Him know He is God of earth too.

- Agree with Him about the sins you may have committed, acknowledging that He has forgiven them.

- Remind God of His promises through His Word, the Bible.

- Present your requests to God. Be specific! Ask for *God's* will to be done—not yours.

- Ask for protection from temptation and from the evil one.

- Thank God *in advance* for the miracles He will work. (This demonstrates your faith.)

- Worship and praise God again, indicating you understand His power and glory.

Some steps the Bible teaches that can help us resist temptation are:

- *Request God's help.* This important portion of the Lord's prayer indicates we need help to not be *led* into temptation. But temptation inevitably occurs. So we also need help to run away from it. This means we also need to resist the evil one, who will constantly try to convince us that wrong things are okay and that his lies are true (John 8:44).

- *Refuse to be intimidated.* God has promised that "he will not let you be tempted beyond what you can bear. But when you are tempted, *he will always provide a way out so that you can stand up under it*" (1 Corinthians 10:13).

- *Refocus your attention.* Temptation's strength is the pull of our own evil desires (our thoughts). These thoughts are what lead to sin (James 1:14,15). Therefore, when our mind is refocused away from evil to good and holy things, temptation can be overcome.

- *Reveal a personal struggle to a friend.* The Bible tells us that two are better than one because when one falls down, the other can help him up (Ecclesiastes 4:10-12).

- *Resist the tempter.* Recognize that your struggle has its ultimate source in the tempter (Satan, along with his demons). The Bible tells us if we submit to God and then resist Satan, he will run (James 4:7). Memorizing Scripture can be a "sword" to use against Satan (Ephesians 6:17). Jesus Himself used Scripture as a "sword" when tempted by Satan in the desert (Matthew 4:1-10).

6. *"For Yours is the kingdom and the power and the glory forever."*

These ending words to the Lord's prayer accomplish the same purpose as the beginning words. They focus us back on God and His ultimate plan for the universe, and on our worship of Him.

Why Do Prayers Seem to Be Answered for Followers of Nonbiblical Religions?

It seems that followers of every religion in the world maintain that some kinds of miracles are performed by a "god" they believe in. Then when they observe such miracles, they proclaim the mightiness of their "god"—and this often keeps them away from the real God of the universe.

Does the Bible Say That Miracles Are Performed by Beings Other Than God?

Yes! Absolutely! It speaks of the existence of the evil one, Satan, and his demons, who can perform miracles.

In the oldest book in the Bible, Job, we find Satan performing incredible miracles to attempt to draw Job away from God. In this account, Satan performed many miracles for evil. For example: 1) He controlled the attackers who slaughtered Job's oxen and servants; 2) he sent fire from heaven, burning up Job's sheep and servants; 3) he sent raiding parties, who stole Job's camels and killed his servants; 4) he sent a powerful wind that caused the house where Job's sons and daughters were to collapse, killing them all; and 5) he inflicted Job with such painful sores all over his body that Job scraped himself with broken pottery (Job 1:13–2:8). Job went from wealth to poverty and from health to sickness. Yet Job remained faithful to the Lord, and was eventually blessed far more than he had been before. God had the ultimate power over Satan.

Why would God allow this? Consider that Job's suffering was temporary when compared with eternity. And today, look at the millions of people who have been given hope by reading about Job.

Or take the miracles duplicated by the Egyptian Pharaoh's magicians in their confrontation with Moses and Aaron: 1) throwing down staffs that became snakes, 2) the plague of blood, and

3) the plague of frogs (Exodus 7:8–8:6). We cannot always understand why God allows Satan to act.

Does Satan Ever Perform "Good" Miracles That People Ask For? Why?

Yes. The Bible tells us, "Satan himself masquerades as an angel of light...and his servants masquerade as *servants of righteousness*" (2 Corinthians 11:14,15). Why would Satan do that? *So he can draw people away from Jesus* by appearing to be a "god." For instance, spiritists often give accounts of miracles. In the United States, we hear about healing miracles from mind science religions (Christian Science and others)—religions whose beliefs are far from biblical doctrine.

It is not necessary for Satan to turn everyone into followers of bizarre satanic cults. Think of it. Just one step off the path to the true God—one step away from believing and accepting the Jesus of the Bible (God incarnate, who died so people could freely accept Him)—accomplishes the objective. Healing miracles can encourage this. *People tend to believe in the miracle instead of believing the Bible and the prophecy that comes from the one God* (Isaiah 46:10). The Bible warns us that such miraculous "signs and wonders" will be performed in the end times:

> "The coming of the lawless one will be in accordance with the work of Satan displayed in all kinds of counterfeit miracles, signs and wonders, and every sort of evil that deceives those who are perishing. *They perish because they refused to love the truth* [the Jesus of the Bible] *and so be saved*."
> —*2 Thessalonians 2:9,10*

So beware of "Christian Scientists" and other nonbiblical "miracle-intensive" religions.

How then do we know the right God to pray to?

> Follow an authority that contains *perfect prophecy*—
> the Bible—and the God revealed in it.

Biblically Based Healing— The Experience of Horace and Millie Willard

Of course the God of the universe can do miracles far beyond Satan—including healing. Jesus healed people paralyzed from birth (Mark 2:1-12), that were blind (Matthew 9:27-30), and that had many other types of maladies. (Jesus' miracles are even referred to in sources other than the Bible.)

The disciples of Jesus were sent out to heal people with many illnesses, using His authority (Matthew 10:1). As His followers, we also can pray and have God grant healing. We do need to remember that healing and other miracles occur only if it's in the will of God. Jesus exemplified this. Sometimes the Father did not allow healing to occur (Mark 6:5). Whether it does or not, the important thing is *God's will*. The counterfeit healings of Satan may draw some people into eternal death, which is far worse than physical death. We must be certain of the "god" we are praying to.

The account of Horace and Millie Willard[10] demonstrates the healing that can occur when Jesus is the authority in people's lives. Horace has been a follower of Jesus for many years. He married his wife Millie in 1941, and they both became Christians in 1949. Since that time, Horace has avidly promoted the good news of Jesus to many people, first using his position as a contractor, and later through Saddleback Church in the Los Angeles area. His passion is obvious. Estimates are that Horace has helped about 10,000 people to a personal relationship with Jesus. Few people could be regarded as more avid followers of Jesus than Horace.

Difficult News

In 1988, Horace's wife Millie became very ill. After going to many specialists, she underwent a heart biopsy. The shocking news was that she had cardiomyopathy, which is essentially irreversible muscle damage to the heart. It was caused by a viral infection of the heart, and there was no cure. Horace and Millie were advised to move to Arizona and await a heart transplant, without which she would surely die. X-rays showed her heart to be much larger than normal; she was to have it checked by x-ray regularly to determine whether drastic action might be necessary.

Doctors indicated that if her heart enlarged any more, it would burst. Precise "ejection fraction" tests showed Millie's blood flow rate to be seriously low—about half of normal. It seemed certain that Millie would get worse and worse and die within a few months. Horace even began making funeral arrangements and determined the pastor for the funeral.

Millie refused the heart transplant and the move to Arizona, preferring instead to have a peaceful death and be with Jesus. So Horace set up a temporary arrangement in their living room where Millie could be elevated (as in a hospital bed) to avoid fluid buildup in her lungs. She was constantly on oxygen, which required Horace and the family to have many tanks available to keep her alive. They took her to the hospital every four days for x-rays, hoping for news that might save her life.

Intervention by Prayer

Horace and many others who were aware of the situation were continually deep in prayer for a long stretch of time. A prayer team at Saddleback Church was involved on a daily basis, as were other prayer partners of the Willards. Like most of us, the Willards wondered whether God would answer their prayers.

About 15 days after returning from the hospital, on the evening of May 20, 1988 (the Willards remember it as if it were yesterday), Horace felt overcome with the situation. He went into their bedroom, dropped to his knees, and began asking God for help in a very passionate and personal way.

He started praying with the following approach: 1) praising God, 2) reminding Him of His promises, 3) outlining the problem, 4) asking for help, and 5) thanking and praising Him in advance for His care. Millie, in a haze of weakness, could hear Horace's words from the other room. His prayer lasted about 20 minutes. In paraphrase, he said:

> "God, I need help. You are the wonderful Creator of the universe who cares for individuals like Millie. It is my desire that you heal Millie. I know that You can heal people because I've read in the Bible that You healed people who were paralyzed and blind. I've read that You even have raised people from the dead. So I pray that You would heal Millie and reveal Yourself and all Your glory with this miracle. I thank You for everything, Father. In Jesus name, amen."

Immediately Horace saw a vision of Millie as if she were on a "large TV screen." She had a "milky like" substance running through her veins. He felt the strong presence of God and knew right then that Millie was being healed by the Holy Spirit. At that point Horace got up and went into the living room, going over to Millie who was still on oxygen and in great pain. Horace announced, "Millie, God has healed you!"

> During my years as a skeptic, I would have totally rejected the idea of something like this!

Unbelievably, Millie sat up, feeling a powerful sensation in her chest. She proclaimed, "Yes, God has healed me." In tears, the couple held each other, recognizing an incredible miracle that only the God of the universe could have performed. The oxygen tubes had fallen from Millie's face when she sat up—and that night she slept peacefully, without oxygen, for the first time since she had been admitted to the hospital. She was never on oxygen again.

On Record with Evidence

The next day, Millie had to go to her heart doctor for her regular x-ray analysis. She proclaimed at the outset that she had been healed by God. The doctor, a skeptical person as I used to be, laughed and said, "OK, let's take the x-rays."

The x-rays showed an incredible change from those taken four days previous. Millie's heart had changed back to a normal size.

And her ejection fraction (blood flow measurement) was back to normal. All of this had occurred over one night. The doctors proclaimed it a miracle. And unlike many healing miracles, which seem to be staged, this one has hard evidence—x-rays from before and after, and ejection fraction flow rates. Since then, Millie has had several echocardiograms (a basic analysis of the heart's condition), and all have indicated that her heart is stronger than it's ever been.[11]

To sum up: First, Millie has the hard evidence of the "before" and "after" x-rays of her heart. No one can refute this. Second, there is the prognosis that she would die soon. Again, the charts reveal this, and it is indisputable. Third, there are witnesses to her sudden recovery. Fourth, she is alive today, over a dozen years later, having far outlasted the doctors' estimates.

Prayers for Needs—
The Experiences of
Rich and Pam Boyer

The Bible tells us that in all things we should pray and look to God (Ephesians 6:18). Note that this is not in some things, but all things. Though we have human desires and wrong human motives, God also puts His desires in our hearts and puts in His good motives. The important thing is to ask God that He would give us desires according to His will, not ours. Then we can feel confident enough to thank Him in advance. Remember that God has promised to fulfill all our needs, but not all our greeds (Matthew 6:33). Yet often we don't receive God's blessings simply because we don't ask, or because we don't ask with the right attitude.

> "If you believe, you will receive whatever
> you ask for in prayer."
> —*Matthew 21:22*

> "Until now you have not asked for anything in my name.
> Ask and you will receive, and your joy will be complete."
> —*Jesus, in John 16:24*

> "When you ask, you do not receive, because you
> ask with the wrong motives, that you may spend what
> you get on your own pleasures."
> —*James 4:3*

Everybody has needs, and virtually everybody prays to someone or something. If you are connected in a right relationship with the right God, in accordance with His timing, your prayers will be answered (1 John 3:21–24). Examine the example of Pam and Rich Boyer below. Their prayer life was intensive, emotional—they prayed with passion to a God they loved. They did not always receive answers to prayer on their timetable, but the answers always came soon enough—on *God's* timetable. God's answers to their prayers are truly amazing and are verifiable.[12]

Rich Prays for a Wife

Rich Boyer was only 19 years old when he determined exactly what kind of woman he wanted to marry. Although young, Rich was mature beyond his years, being the youngest person ever, at the time, to pass the CPA exam in the state of California. He used an accountant's analytical thinking in praying for his future wife. He asked God that she have the following "specifications":

1. She was to be shorter than he (Rich is five-foot-six)

2. She was to be a brunette

3. She was to be four years younger than he was

4. She was to love music (Rich is a musician)

   ...and to ultimately confirm God's selection...

5. She was to have exactly the same birthdate as Rich

Five years after that prayer, in January of 1973, Rich met Pam. She was a five-foot-tall brunette who was four years younger than Rich. They first met at the Edgewater Hyatt House in Long Beach, California, at the prompting of several rowdy friends of Rich's. Pam had felt prompted by God to work there on the graveyard shift, despite the heavy-drinking customers.

Early in their courtship, Rich noticed an emerald ring on Pam's hand. He asked her if it was perhaps something related to a May birthday, which Pam affirmed it was. Naturally, the follow-up question from Rich was, what date was Pam born? And of course the answer was on May 6, exactly four years after Rich. They were married on August 11, 1973.

God answers prayers for spouses. Not always. And not always specifically, as with Rich and Pam. But we can trust God to provide according to His ultimate purpose.

Prayers for a Piano

No one suggests that we pray for our "greeds," but sometimes when our hearts are filled with a desire, it is from God. That's why the Bible tells us to pray in *all* things (Ephesians 6:18). Often these desires turn out to be part of the plans of God.

As an accomplished musician, though young and with virtually no money, Rich wanted a grand piano. In fact he wanted a nice one, a Steinway that would be in mahogany (extremely rare), to complement his decor. This was normally a special order that would take two years on a waiting list and would cost considerably over $10,000 (worth considerably more in 1975 than now!). Although this was a totally unrealistic dream for the young couple, the two decided to pray that God would provide it.

Within weeks, Rich was involved in helping a couple with some accounting work. They had heard him play the piano. They then asked him if he would be willing to "house" a piano they had in storage—one they couldn't fit into their home. Rich of course agreed and asked what kind of piano. The couple replied that it was a Steinway grand. "It wouldn't happen to be mahogany, would it?" Rich asked. "Yes, it is mahogany—how did you know?" was their response. *God provides.*

Rich used the incredible mahogany piano at a new Bible study that was started to help musicians know Jesus. It was a central part of their worship. Several of the previously very rough musicians came to accept Jesus. Others grew to know Him better. God

honored the extravagant desire of two poor newlyweds for a greater purpose—to bring others to Him. And He revealed His glory and His influence over even the daily matters and details of life.

Prayer Rescues the Contents of a Shoebox

The Orange County Rescue Mission was building a new facility in downtown Santa Ana, California, one of the most crime-ridden areas of the nation. The contractor had misestimated his costs and was $30,000 short of the money needed to pay bills that were due immediately. At an emergency meeting of the board of directors, after all the fundraising options were discussed, Rich Boyer spoke up and said that the one thing they had not done was to simply ask God to provide the funds. Rob Martin, director of the mission, agreed. The group left the meeting deep in prayer, without having any other plan to resolve the problem of the $30,000 shortfall.

The next morning, as the mission's secretary walked by a few people who were waiting for the welfare office across the street to open, she noticed a curious thing—a shoebox had been left at the front of the newly constructed rescue mission. Opening the box, she found ten gold  Krugerrands, three bars of silver, and several old coins. When Rob Martin arrived, he immediately called the police and the mayor to report the finding of the valuables. He was informed that if nobody reported the items missing within seven hours, they were the property of the finding party. No one did.

Then Rob called the Monex Company in Newport Beach (a nearby town), who appraised them at $30,056 and then purchased them on the spot. It was precisely the amount needed to pay the rescue mission's bills, just a day after the board had prayed for that amount. Who was the "Santa Claus"? Or, more accurately in this case, who was God's agent? None of the board would have been motivated or had the means to do such a thing. Nobody knows to this day how the box got there. God is powerful.

Prayers for Guidance—
The Experience of Rick and Kay
Warren and Saddleback Church

Answers to prayer are not limited to healing and the other miracles already mentioned. Perhaps the most effective use of prayer is for guidance—before a crisis erupts or simply to direct us in everyday life. The Bible says that people are foolish to trust themselves, but are safe if they use wisdom (Proverbs 28:26). A moving example of answered prayer for guidance is the story of Rick and Kay Warren, who started Saddleback Church—now one of the largest churches in the United States.[13]

In 1973, Saddleback Church did not exist. Its future pastor, Rick Warren, was only 19 years old. He was not married, nor had he met his future wife, Kay. Though Rick felt called to some kind of work with Christians, he didn't necessarily envision himself becoming a pastor. Yet in one moment of prayer (see "Arrow Prayer" insert on page 20) at a lecture by Dr. W.A. Criswell— a highly esteemed man of God—in November, 1973, Rick prayed to commit himself to becoming a pastor.

God immediately confirmed his prayer. When Rick and a friend finally got through a long line to shake the pastor's hand, Criswell looked into Rick's eyes and exclaimed, "Young man, I feel led to lay hands on you and pray for you." The resulting prayer was that Rick would receive a "double portion" of God's spirit, and that the church Rick would pastor would grow to double the size of Criswell's church—which was then the largest Baptist church in the world. Little did Rick know at the time what the extent of God's plans for this calling was, and what his short "arrow" prayer would mean to his life and the lives of millions of others.

Start with Prayer for Guidance

So often people put off prayer until a crisis. Then they may say, "Well, I guess all we can do now is pray." As we have already seen, the great leaders in the Bible put prayer *first*. God wants people to seek Him and talk to Him *ahead of time*—to listen, to put our trust in Him. We should pray for guidance and direction before the inevitable problems come up. And such prayers for guidance can direct "ordinary people" to extraordinary results. Note the example of Rick and Kay Warren's history of prayer for guidance before facing a seemingly insurmountable challenge.

Rick and Kay were married in June 1975. They were students with little money—Rick was just about to complete his final year at Southwestern Baptist Seminary in Fort Worth, Texas. Being committed to following God's will, they prayed for *six months* about how and where Rick would pastor a church. Using the biblical prayer model (see pages 20–27), Rick joined with his wife in prayer, seeing her participation as a key element in discerning God's will.

Rick had been a missionary in Japan, and he wanted to start a church abroad. But constant impressions and confirmation from God led the couple to determine that Rick should start a church in a U.S. metropolitan area, with the purpose of attracting non-Christians, building them up in spiritual maturity, and finally sending them out on missions. To this end, Rick and Kay posted a map in their small apartment and prayed about God's intended location for the church. God led them to Orange County, California.

Don't Underestimate God

It's easy to unthinkingly put human limitations on God and place a "box" around Him. But the Bible teaches us that *nothing* is impossible with God (Matthew 17:20; Luke 1:37). So picture a young couple about to leave Texas to start a new church in an area they knew little about, with no money and no staff. It was a move that required faith in God and in everything He has said.

How many people would venture into an unknown land or into unknown circumstances based totally on faith? Abraham did. Nehemiah did. The Bible teaches that faith pleases God if it's based on real belief in Him and in earnestly seeking Him (Hebrews 11:6). Rick and Kay took that step of faith, leaving

Texas with virtually no resources to start a church in an area they had never seen, only researched—Saddleback Valley. Months of prayer had guided them.

Upon arriving, their first concern was to find a place to live. A God that created the universe could certainly provide them shelter. The very first real estate office the couple pulled into found them a condominium despite the fact they had no money for a normal down payment. And the real estate agent, Don Dale, became the church's very first member.

Where God Guides, God Provides

Any startup organization needs resources, be it a church or a business. In the case of Saddleback Church, a prudent person would have asked where the resources were to come from. After all, Rick and Kay had virtually no money and no staff. Yet the Bible teaches us that *if we trust God* with our time and our money, our blessings will overflow (Malachi 3:10). Rick and Kay trusted God. When money was tight, they still kept giving the same portion of their income to the church. When time was tight, they still allocated time for God. Staying deep in prayer right from the outset of the work, Rick and Kay prayed for God's will to be done. They followed God's prompting without reservation and received God's blessings.

God Provides Saddleback Church

Few people would have expected the miracles from God that Rick and Kay Warren literally assumed would happen because of prayer. The Bible teaches us that such faith—assuming God's response—is vital to a healthy prayer life. It can "move mountains" (Matthew 17:20).

On March 30, 1980, Rick Warren stood up before the first, tiny public audience in the new Saddleback Church and boldly announced Saddleback Church's future based on his prayers:

Saddleback Church would become a place...

1. Where depressed, frustrated, and confused people could find love and acceptance.

2. Where the people of Orange County would hear the gospel of Jesus.

3. Where 20,000 members would be welcomed into a fellowship of harmony.

4. Where people would be developed into maturity.

5. Where believers would learn to use the gifts that God had given them.

6. Where hundreds of career missionaries would be based and from which thousands of short-term missionaries would spread the gospel.

7. Where at least 50 acres of land would house a regional site for worship in Orange County, including many facilities for spiritual development.

Rick concluded by saying, "I stand before you today and state in *confident assurance* that these dreams will become reality. Why? Because they are inspired by God."[13]

Was this risky? In the time of Moses, God commanded that people speaking falsely in His name be put to death (Deuteronomy 18:20). With a church of only 15 people in 1980, this dream would seem to have been impossible. Now, only a couple decades later, Saddleback Church has well over 20,000 attendees and has more than 50 acres of well-situated property to help it accomplish its goals. It has developed many sister churches and is sending thousands of people on missions around the world. Worldwide, it is considered a church model. Rick and Kay's prayers were precisely answered.

Prayers Fulfilled in My Life

As a former skeptic myself, I expect that many skeptics will disregard the statements I make about my own answers to prayers (I certainly would have—but now I've actually experienced them). But this skepticism doesn't make the prayers and answers less valid. So I would be remiss to not review some of the many incredible answers to prayer I have experienced.

Many people have been involved in guiding me, and I've discovered that God's guidance comes not only from the Bible and from Bible teachers, but also from Christian friends and Bible-based TV and radio broadcasts. You never know when God is going to talk to you! Prayers in all the categories we've discussed—healing, needs, and guidance—have been answered in my own life.

Prayers for Healing

A number of years ago, shortly after I became a Christian, my family and I lost a tremendous amount of wealth. Perhaps it was God's means of cleansing my sinful life. Perhaps it was just the consequence of my own prideful mistakes. Whatever the case was, the rapid loss of a very great amount of wealth, to the point where I faced the specter of destitution, caused a period of severe depression for me—the type of depression that causes many people to commit sui

As a new Christian, it would have been easy for me to retreat and give up. Instead, based on what I had already learned about the reality of Jesus and God's omnipotence and love (exactly what I write about in the *Examine the Evidence* Series), I prayed for strength and healing. I remember well the days I struggled immensely just to get out of bed to go look for a job, and the days I thought my mind would never be healed. I remember lying in bed, my wife at my side, feeling like a total failure and wondering what the future would bring. I remember being very anxious even in very minor social situations, despite my lengthy past life as a high-level executive who was constantly involved in socializing. I remember how my head would hurt—I remember questioning whether it would ever get well. I remember thinking, *Is this what Christianity is all about?* But I continued to read the Bible and pray. The doctors indicated that had it not been for my "resolve" (my faith), I probably would never have recovered.

Sometimes when God is preparing to do important things in someone's life, there are spiritual attacks from Satan, who will do whatever he can to thwart progress. I thank God that, through the support of Saddleback Church and the encouragement from my own studies, I recognized the reality of my evil opponent and understood his tactics. I prayed very often. After three years, I was healed from the debilitating depression. Not only did I regain my mind, but I gained a new understanding of the suffering that people go through and a new trust in the power of prayer. God answered my prayers according to His overall purpose. He was preparing me for the work I'm now engaged in (Romans 8:28).

Prayers for Needs

Rebuilding a life after losing great wealth and descending into poverty is difficult. In some ways, it may be more difficult than not having wealth in the first place. Though it would not be fair to compare this experience to the misery of a life in a ghetto, yet from a mental standpoint, when a person places his security in money, but then loses it and faces the specter of homelessness, he can literally go crazy. The rich tend to rely on *wealth*, the poor tend to rely on *God*. If the rich don't have God, when financial disaster strikes, they often take their own lives. Jesus said that the meek would inherit the earth, which I never understood until we became poor. God prepared me for this—through my own prayers that "broke me," causing me to focus on Him. Now I rely on God for our needs, not my bank account.

I clearly remember one day when my wife, Jan, came home weeping because she couldn't find a home to live in—after weeks of searching. Though we occupied a very large house, the real estate market had crashed, and we had to move very quickly. We had been praying for many things. I was focusing on finding employment, and Jan was focusing on finding a home.

But neither of us had been successful. I'll never forget telling my wife not to worry (right!), then jumping in a car and sending a quick prayer to God that we really needed a home—fast! (See "Arrow Prayers" on page 20.) The very first place I saw was a house that the owner was willing to lease to us with no down payment and in total acceptance of our situation. Despite weeks of searching by my wife, when it came down to the final few hours in which we had to move out, God provided a home within an hour. Prayer is the only thing I can attribute it to.

Many other obstacles had to be faced after our sudden financial disaster. In southern California it's virtually impossible to keep certain types of employment without an automobile. When both husband and wife work, that means *two* automobiles. We were forced into a one-car situation with almost no funds to purchase a second automobile, and my consulting required extensive driving. After several nights of prayer by my family, one of my sons located a 1984 Volvo we could purchase for only $500. It "just happened" to be owned by a member of Saddleback Church. The car was not very appealing, and the odometer had "frozen" at 168,000 miles. Interestingly, it already had the "fish" sign of Jesus on its back end.

We bought the car, and it became one of the best purchases of our lives. After about six years and at least another hundred thousand miles, the car continued to perform well in every way. Lots of miles...abuse...it seemed that nothing could break that car! Today, my wife and I still laugh about how we would turn to one side to avoid the inevitable "sunroof drenching"—water pouring all over the driver—after it rained. The only repair that was required in all those years was a new fuel pump. Finally we sold it to another Christian who was desperate as we had been, for immediate, very inexpensive transportation. He said this had answered his prayers, as it had ours. We took a picture so we could remember that beloved car.

Prayers for God's Guidance

We experienced many fulfilled prayers that provided for my Christian work and for our family. Dozens of people would attest to this. When we needed people, they would show up unexpectedly. When we needed money, it would

The author and his family with their "miracle car.

come unexpectedly. When we needed help of any kind, it would "just appear." We just prayed for help. We've learned to expect it.

One of my most memorable experiences was with God's guidance. In early 1996 I felt overwhelmed by the enormous amount of time I was spending in four areas that I was focusing on. I prayed, asking God to remove any areas He didn't want me to be involved in. (This was a risky prayer.) Within two weeks, all my income-producing jobs disappeared. The only thing left was a two-book test I was doing for this Christian effort—the books that became the start of the *Examine the Evidence* Series.

I had absolutely no staff or money with which to create a publishing enterprise. I prayed again and said, "Okay, God, if this is what you really want me to do, you'll have to provide." I decided to dedicate myself not to the business world of my past, but to writing, publishing, speaking, and teaching about the Bible that I had rejected as a skeptic. This created some difficulty because my wife was used to the more "assured" income we had been receiving from major companies. But God encouraged us and helped us.

Within a week, I got a call from a major design firm in Orange County, Synergy Incorporated, that had seen my primitive self-published books. They offered to design book covers and marketing materials at no cost. Since then they have contributed at least $20,000 in free design to the work. I continued to receive invaluable advice and mentoring from Mark Swenson of Sonshine Christian Store, who had helped me with the test marketing for the books. At the same time a distributor agreed to an arrangement that allowed the publishing effort to get off the ground. Dozens of other prayers were answered, enabling books to be printed, displays to be manufactured, and the series to be distributed. Unexpected donations helped support my family's modest life-style. (Businessmen would never believe that such an uncapitalized publishing effort could make it!)

We are still praying to erase some final debt that allowed us to start the work. We know that God will provide. Most importantly, our prayers for our ministry have been answered, with many people coming to know Jesus as a result of accepting God's invitation to follow Him.

Common Questions

Wouldn't a Loving God Allow Good People into Heaven?

Many people believe that living a good life and being kind to others is the way to heaven. Naturally, they are thinking of a "good" life in terms of our distorted human view; and such a life is far from God's standard. The Bible says that the *only* way to God the Father in heaven is through Jesus Christ (John 14:6). So will loving and "good" people who don't accept Jesus go to hell? Yes—but how can they be truly good if they reject the love of God's Son, Jesus, who died for them?

God will allow perfectly good people into heaven. But His standard of goodness is the perfection of His Son, Jesus. Hence, there is simply no other way to come to Him except through Jesus—let alone the fact that every sin of mind or body we commit removes us further from Jesus' perfection (Matthew 5:28,29; Romans 3:22,23).

Everyone is imperfect, but the good news is that God has provided Jesus as a perfect sacrifice for us. He is our only way to heaven. Not accepting God's gift of love and forgiveness through Jesus, despite the Holy Spirit's prompting, is unforgivable (Mark 3:29).

How Can We Ensure the Right Relationship So We Can Go to Heaven?

When Jesus said that not all who use His name will enter heaven (Matthew 7:21-23), He was referring to people who think using Christ' name along with rules and rituals is the key to heaven. A *relationship* with God is not based on rituals or rules. It's based on grace, forgiveness, and the right standing with Him through Jesus Christ.

How to Have a Personal Relationship with God

1. *Believe that God exists* and that He came to earth in the human form of Jesus Christ (John 3:16; Romans 10:9).

2. *Accept God's free forgiveness of sins and gift of new life* through the death and resurrection of Jesus Christ (Ephesians 2:8-10; 1:7,8).

3. *Switch to God's plan for your life* (1 Peter 1:21-23; Ephesians 2:1-7).

4. *Expressly make Jesus Christ the Director* of your life (Matthew 7:21-27 1 John 4:15).

Prayer for Eternal Life with God

"Dear God, I believe You sent Your Son, Jesus, to die for my sins so I can be forgiven. I'm sorry for my sins, and I want to live the rest of my life the way You want me to. Please put Your Spirit in my life to direct me. Amen."

Then What?

People who sincerely take these steps become members of God's family of believers. A new world of freedom and strength is available through Jesus' life within you, expressing itself through prayer and obedience to God's will. The new relationship can be strengthened by taking the following steps:

- Find a Bible-based church that you like and attend regularly.
- Set aside some time each day to pray and read the Bible.
- Locate other Christians to spend time with on a regular basis.

God's Promises to Believers

For Today

"Seek first his kingdom and his righteousness, and all these things [things to satisfy all your needs] will be given to you as well."
—Matthew 6:33

For Eternity

"Whoever believes in the Son has eternal life, but whoever rejects the Son will not see life, for God's wrath remains on him."
—John 3:36

Once we develop an eternal perspective, even the greatest problems on earth fade in significance.

Notes

1. Behe, Michael J., *Darwin's Black Box*, New York, NY: The Free Press, 1996.

2. Muncaster, Ralph O., *Creation vs. Evolution*, Eugene, OR: Harvest House, 2000.

3. Ross, Hugh, Ph.D., *Facts & Faith* newsletter, Fourth Quarter, 1996.

4. Muncaster, Ralph O., *Does the Bible Predict the Future?*, Eugene, OR: Harvest House, 2000.

5. Muncaster, Ralph O., *How Do We Know Jesus Is God?*, Eugene, OR: Harvest House, 2000.

6. Muncaster, Ralph O., *Science—Was the Bible Ahead of Its Time?*, Eugene, OR: Harvest House, 2000.

7. Muncaster, Ralph O., *Can You Trust the Bible?*, Eugene, OR: Harvest House, 2000.

8. Muncaster, Ralph O., *What Is the Proof for the Resurrection?*, Eugene, OR: Harvest House, 2000.

9. Warren, Rick, *God's Answer to Your Needs*, Foothill Ranch, CA: Encouraging Word, 1999.

10. Willard, Horace and Millie, personal interview with the author, Dec. 4, 2000.

11. Willard, Gary, MD, personal interview with the author, Dec. 7, 2000.

12. Boyer, Rich and Pam, personal interview with the author, Dec. 2, 2000.

13. Warren, Rick, *The Purpose-Driven Church*, Grand Rapids, MI: Zondervan Publishing House, 1995; and Rick Warren, many talks and presentations heard personally by the author, 1988–2000.

Bibliography

Elwell, Walter A. (Editor), *Evangelical Dictionary of Theology*, Grand Rapids, MI: Baker Book House Co., 1984.

Geisler, Norman, Ph.D., and Brooks, Ron, *When Skeptics Ask*, Grand Rapids, MI: Baker Books, 1990.

Life Application Bible, Wheaton, IL: Tyndale House Publishers, and Grand Rapids, MI: Zondervan Publishing House, 1991.

Lockyer, Herbert, *All the Miracles of the Bible*, Grand Rapids, MI: Zondervan Publishing House, 1961.

McDowell, Josh, *Handbook of Today's Religions*, San Bernardino, CA: Campus Crusade for Christ, 1983.

McDowell, Josh, and Wilson, Bill, *A Ready Defense*, San Bernardino, CA: Here's Life Publishers, Inc., 1990.

Muncaster, Ralph O., *How Can We Be Certain We Are Going to Heaven?*, Eugene, OR: Harvest House, 2001.

Muncaster, Ralph O., *What Makes Jesus Different from Other Religious Leaders?*, Eugene, OR: Harvest House, 2001.

Smith, F. LaGard, *The Daily Bible In Chronological Order*, Eugene, OR: Harvest House, 1984.

Walvoord, John F., *The Prophecy Knowledge Handbook*, Wheaton, IL: Victor Books, 1990.

Youngblood, Ronald F., *New Illustrated Bible Dictionary*, Nashville, TN: Nelson, 1995.

Zodhiates, Spiros, *The Complete Word Study of the New Testament*, Chattanooga, TN: AMG Publishers, 1991.

Zodhiates, Spiros, *The Complete Word Study of the Old Testament*, Chattanooga, TN: AMG Publishers, 1994.